FOR A

Brilliant

BROTHER

summersdale

FOR A BRILLIANT BROTHER

Copyright © Summersdale Publishers Ltd, 2013

Illustrations © Shutterstock

Summersdale Publishers Ltd
46 West Street
Chichester
West Sussex
PO19 1RP
UK

www.summersdale.com

Printed and bound in China

ISBN: 978-1-84953-339-3

Substantial discounts on bulk quantities of Summersdale books are available to corporations, professional associations and other organisations. For details telephone Nicky Douglas on (+44-1243-756902), fax (+44-1243-786300) or email (nicky@summersdale.com).

To......................................

From..................................

All for one and one for all.
My brother and my friend.
What fun we have. The
time we share. Brothers
'til the end.

ANONYMOUS

Half the time when brothers wrestle, it's just an excuse to hug each other.

JAMES PATTERSON

When brothers agree, no fortress is so strong as their common life.

ANTISTHENES

The surname of famous videogame brothers Mario and Luigi is Mario, meaning Mario's full name is Mario Mario.

Your siblings are the only people in the world who know what it's like to have been brought up the way you were.

BETSY COHEN

You're brilliant because...

... you always let me play
with your coolest toys.

*It was nice growing up
with someone like you
— someone to lean on,
someone to count on...
someone to tell on!*

ANONYMOUS

A friend loveth at all times, and a brother is born for adversity.

PROVERBS 17:17

*You deserve
an award for:*

Most Reliable
Entertainer during
moments of boredom.

Families are the compass that guides us.

DALAI LAMA

A family in harmony will prosper in everything.

CHINESE PROVERB

Having a close relationship with your brother in early adulthood has been shown to lead to greater physical and mental well-being later in life.

I, who have no sisters or brothers, look with some degree of innocent envy on those who may be said to be born to friends.

JAMES BOSWELL

You're brilliant because...

. . . you always pick me
to be on your team.

The understanding of atomic physics is child's play, compared with the understanding of child's play.

DAVID KRESH

. . . to know how your girl will treat you after marriage, just listen to her talking to her little brother.

SAM LEVENSON

The highlight of my childhood was making my brother laugh so hard that food came out of his nose.

GARRISON KEILLOR

*You deserve
an award for:*

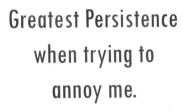

Greatest Persistence
when trying to
annoy me.

The strength of a family, like the strength of an army, is in its loyalty to each other.

MARIO PUZO

A brother is a friend given by Nature.

JEAN BAPTISTE LEGOUVE

Siblings are... the people who teach us about fairness and cooperation and kindness and caring — quite often the hard way.

PAMELA DUGDALE

Research has shown that once a child has reached the age of 11, they have spent approximately 33 per cent of their free time with their sibling.

There is no such thing as fun for the whole family.

JERRY SEINFELD

You're brilliant because...

... you can fix anything.

Happiness is having a large, loving, caring, close-knit family in another city.

GEORGE BURNS

We do not cease to play because we grow old. We grow old because we cease to play.

GEORGE BEARNARD SHAW

You deserve an award for:

Putting Up With Me
through thick and thin.

After a girl is grown, her little brothers — now her protectors — seem like big brothers.

TERRI GUILLEMETS

. . . love is the oil that eases friction, the cement that binds closer together, and the music that brings harmony.

JIM ROHN ON FAMILY LIFE

Younger brothers are shorter on average than their older brothers. However, this is balanced out by the fact that younger brothers find it easier to be creative and adventurous.

The family is one of
nature's masterpieces.

GEORGE SANTAYANA

You're brilliant because...

... you're always on the ball.

O brother man! fold to thy heart thy brother.

JOHN GREENLEAF WHITTIER

Sibling relationships...
outlast marriages, survive
the death of parents,
resurface after quarrels
that would sink any
friendship.

ERICA E. GOODE

. . . my brothers acted like they didn't care, but I always knew they looked out for me and were there!

CATHERINE PULSIFER

You deserve an award for:

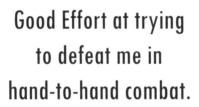

Good Effort at trying to defeat me in hand-to-hand combat.

Being pretty on the inside means you don't hit your brother and you eat all your peas.

LORD CHESTERFIELD

Everyone knows that if you've got a brother, you're going to fight.

LIAM GALLAGHER

It takes two men to make one brother.

ISRAEL ZANGWILL

Famous brothers include the Wright Brothers (Orville and Wilbur, aviation pioneers), the Brothers Grimm (Jacob and Wilhelm, folk tale collectors), and Brian, Carl and Dennis Wilson of the band The Beach Boys.

The best way to get a puppy is to beg for a baby brother — and they'll settle for a puppy every time.

WINSTON PENDELTON

You're brilliant because...

... you always offer
to pick up the bill.

You don't choose your family. They are God's gift to you, as you are to them.

DESMOND TUTU

I've a pretty large experience of boys, and you're a bad set of fellows.

CHARLES DICKENS, GREAT EXPECTATIONS

*You deserve
an award for:*

Outstanding Childhood
Companion.

I always wanted a little brother because I felt like the little brother had to do everything.

PAUL PIERCE

*Affliction's sons are
brothers in distress;
A brother to relieve, how
exquisite the bliss!*

ROBERT BURNS,
'A WINTER NIGHT'

Having a brother might inspire you to be different from him. Research has shown that some children subconsciously differentiate themselves from their sibling by carving out an opposing identity to reduce rivalry.

*He is my most beloved
friend and my bitterest
rival. . . and scariest of
all, my equal.*

GREGG LEVOY

You're brilliant because...

... sometimes you let me win.

When you deal with your brother, be pleasant, but get a witness.

HESIOD

There's no other love like
the love for a brother.
There's no other love like
the love from a brother.

ASTRID ALAUDA

A brother shares childhood memories and grown-up dreams.

 ANONYMOUS

You deserve an award for:

Standing Up For
Me at school.

We are not only our brother's keeper; in countless large and small ways, we are our brother's maker.

BONARO OVERSTREET

Brothers and sisters are as close as hands and feet.

VIETNAMESE PROVERB

*God blesses him who
helps his brother.*

ABU BAKR

Much of a child's social skills in later life depend upon their interaction with siblings. Through a brother or sister, they can learn how to manage disagreements and regulate their emotions.

What are little boys
made of?
Frogs and snails
And puppy-dogs' tails,
That's what little boys
are made of.

NURSERY RHYME

You're brilliant because...

... you always know when it's
time to get the drinks in.

*There is a destiny that
makes us brothers:
None goes his way alone:
All that we send into the
lives of others
Comes back onto our own.*

EDWIN MARKHAM,
'A CREED'

Children of the same family, the same blood, with the same first associations and habits, have some means of enjoyment in their power, which no subsequent connections can supply...

JANE AUSTEN

*You deserve
an award for:*

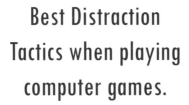

Best Distraction
Tactics when playing
computer games.

Help your brother's boat across, and your own will reach the shore.

HINDU PROVERB

Our brothers and sisters are there with us from the dawn of our personal stories to the inevitable dusk.

SUSAN SCARF MERRELL

A study has shown that women with older brothers are more likely to initiate a conversation with a male stranger and will smile at him more frequently than he smiles at her.

I sought my soul, but my soul I could not see. I sought my God, but my God eluded me. I sought my brother and I found all three.

ANONYMOUS

You're brilliant because...

... you make the best
midnight snacks.

To the outside world we all grow old. But not to brothers and sisters. We know each other as we always were.

CLARA ORTEGA

If thy brother wrongs thee, remember not so much his wrong-doing, but more than ever that he is thy brother.

EPICTETUS

Sometimes being a
brother is even better
than being a superhero.

MARC BROWN

You deserve an award for:

Astonishing Levels
of Forgiveness.

She took care of her little brother like he was her own son. She always looked out for him.

SARA CRUZ

The family is the country of the heart.

GIUSEPPE MAZZINI

According to a study, older brothers tend to have a higher IQ than their younger brothers, exceeding their IQ scores by an average of 2.3 points.

Brothers don't necessarily have to say anything to each other — they can sit in a room and be together and just be completely comfortable with each other.

LEONARDO DICAPRIO

Nothing can stop me from loving my brother.

BRANDY NORWOOD

You're brilliant because...

... you have the best
taste in music.

A friend is a brother was once a bother.

ANONYMOUS

Sisterhood and brotherhood is a condition people have to work at.

MAYA ANGELOU

You deserve an award for:

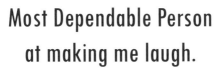

Most Dependable Person
at making me laugh.

Never make a companion equal to a brother.

HESIOD

You're brilliant because...

... you're always at the other end of the line when I need you.

If you're interested in finding out more about our gift books follow us on Twitter: **@Summersdale**

www.summersdale.com